How to be a Great

Great

WIFE

...even though you homeschool

How to be a Great WIFE

...even though you homeschool

TODD WILSON

FM Publishing
Milford, IN

ISBN 10 Digit: 1-933858-38-9
ISBN 13 Digit: 978-1-933858-38-8

Printed in the United States of America

To my beloved bride,

Thanks for hanging on my arm and cheering me on. It sure isn't easy being married to me or traveling the country in an RV with eight children. You've done it without complaint...OK, without much complaint. Also, you know I couldn't be what I was created to be without you.

I need you and love you,
~ Me

Contents

Introduction

FOR THE LAST couple years, my family and I have traveled parts of the country encouraging homeschooling moms and dads. Besides all of our RV adventures, I've had the pleasure of speaking to thousands of men and women in workshops, seminars, and one on one.

This book was born out of one of those wokshops. I am still amazed at the overwhelming response to the very important message of being a homeschooling wife rather than a homeschooling mom.

In my workshops, women laugh and cry, and often corner me afterwards and ask, "How can I get my husband more involved in our family?" This book is my answer to that question.

So, I invite you to laugh, nod your head, and...cry as you read this book. (Well, you're a woman, right?) Within these pages, you'll find comfort and reassurance that you're not alone in what you feel. My purpose in writing this book is not to make you feel guilty as a wife. You've read enough books that do that...in fact, throw those books away!

My desire is to show you how to get your husband more involved in your family, in your marriage, and in home educating your children. Every woman wants her husband more involved; it's universal.

I would just about guess that you believe what most homeschooling moms believe: that everyone else's marriage is better than yours and that every other husband is more involved.

That's a lie. The truth is, everyone struggles in marriage, my wife and I included. My wife believes the lie as well. She looks around at other couples and assumes that everyone else is happily married and that we're the only ones who struggle. In fact, if she met you today, she'd believe your marriage is great...and you'd probably believe the same about ours. That's just the way it is with women.

Let me set the record straight once and for all. If you're married, you struggle.

So, here's a warning and the reason for reading a book like this: **homeschooling makes the struggle even greater.**

The Danger of Homeschooling

Not long ago, I was being interviewed on the radio by a woman interviewer. As I talked about my recent book, "Help! I'm Married to a Homeschooling Mom," she mentioned that she had homeschooled four of her children all the way through high school.

I was just about to congratulate her, when she added that she was now a divorced, single mom. Without my asking, she went on to say that the main reason for her divorce was because she had spent so many years pouring her life into homeschooling, at the expense of her husband and their marriage.

Now her mission is to sound the alarm to other homeschooling moms that they better not neglect their husbands.

This is a sad story, and an all too common one. The homeschooling world is filled with moms who are pouring their lives into homeschooling their children at the expense of their marriage.

Part of the reason is because homeschooling is like a black hole.

The Black Hole

Somewhere out in deep space, lurks a dark monster that consumes everything in its path. Scientists call it a black hole, but they have never actually seen one. Apparently, some scientist was watching stars through his giant telescope and saw some really black spots in space.

After some testing, the smart scientist settled on this explanation: A long time ago a big star got sick, died, and then shrunk in size. As it shrunk, its mass increased and began to suck in space debris...which increased its mass and its pull even more...which sucked in other space stuff...which increased its mass and its pull, until it was sucking in everything that got too near it.

Scientists believe that the pull towards this dead star is so great that not even light can escape its pull, thereby creating a "black hole" in space.

Homeschooling can be that black hole.

It demands everything. If allowed to go unchecked, it will suck up your strength, hobbies, free time, friendships, and tragically, even your marriage.

It's understandable how this can happen. You feel responsible. You constantly wonder if you're doing a good enough job and often feel like you're letting down your kids. You worry if the curriculum is effective and if your child is getting "it." You lie awake in bed at night and wonder how you can make it another day. You're tired, worn out, and overwhelmed.

You have a list of books to read, tests to give, and a pile of papers to grade. You get together with your homeschooling friends and talk about homeschooling. You have homeschooling dreams (also known as nightmares). You think homeschooling thoughts, look at homeschooling magazines, and attend homeschooling conferences.

If you are totally honest, even during an intimate time with your husband (on some rare occasion), you find yourself thinking about...you guessed it, HOMESCHOOLING.

You've been sucked into the homeschooling hole!

The bad thing about the hole is that when you've been pulled into it, your husband pulls away from you. Just when you need him the most, he seems to be a galaxy away.

You want him to take a more active role and beg him to be more involved in your family and school, but he drifts further away until he is a stranger in your own house.

You read books (that's why you're reading this one), you nag or try to be more gentle but nothing works. Your heart aches for oneness, but you've given up hope that things will ever change. So you trudge along doing it all yourself...and you're about to crumble.

Even the idea of having to work harder at your marriage is defeating. You think, "I don't have time to work harder at my marriage...I'm tired and the kids aren't getting any younger, and if I give time to him, I won't be able to get all the schooling done..."

OK, stop right now and take a deep breath.

Feel better?

Well, let's change subjects for a few minutes and talk about...plants.

The Stem and the Leaves

I love plants. I like big specimen trees, towering evergreens, antique perennials, and dazzling annuals. In fact, I've probably planted thousands of flowers in my lifetime. My technique is fast and easy. I take a flat of flowers, push my finger into the bottom of the plastic cell, grab the plant firmly by the stem, pluck it from the container, and plop it in the ground in a matter of seconds.

I should say, that **was** my technique before a master gardener on PBS rocked my landscaping world. I was watching his gardening show one Saturday morning as he (Roger Swaine, for all you PBS groupies) described the best way to pull a flower from its plastic container. I looked on, dumbfounded, as he pulled the plant out of the container by its leaves.

"That's the dumbest thing I've ever heard," I said outloud to the screen.

The master gardener then went on to describe the reasoning behind his madness. He explained that if you pull a plant out by the leaves and accidentally yank off a leaf or two, it wouldn't hurt the plant. But, if you pull a plant by the stem and accidentally damage it, the plant will die.

He's right.

Think of your marriage as the stem of the homeschooling plant. All the other things...curriculum, lesson plans, math facts, schedules, and programs...are all leaves. If you mess those up, overlook them, or ignore them accidentally (or on purpose), it won't be the end of the world.

However, if you neglect your marriage, overlook it, or put it on hold, you run the very real risk of bruising the stem. If you ruin the stem, all your best efforts will not save the plant.

Let's take the illustration a step further. If you nurture the stem, allowing it to grow strong, you assure the health and success of the plant. Translation: *Take care of your marriage and homeschooling will take care of itself.*

In the following pages, I would like to share with you what every husband wants and what happens when those 'wants' aren't met. Now, before you toss the book out the window, let me say that I'm going to make the concept very easy for you to remember.

I'm going to give you the keys to a successful marriage and homeschool all wrapped up into one, easy-to-remember, 12-word phrase (but you're going to have to wait until the last chapter to find out what it is).

Before we talk about the specific wants of your husband and why meeting them is so important, let's take a look at the word 'wants'.

CHAPTER 1

Desires of the Heart

BASICALLY, 'WANTS' ARE the desires and cravings of every living creature. For example, my dog, Chewy (a Chihuahua with issues), wants two things in life: table scraps and affection. I mean he craves them with an intense desire.

When he hears the clink of a spoon on a plate, his ears stand up straight, and he makes a beeline to the source of the noise, hoping that something will fall his direction.

As far as affection goes, the dumb dog can't get enough. If you stopped by our house, he'd be on your lap in two shakes of his whisker. If you didn't push him away, he'd inch his way closer to your face until he was perched on your head. He just 'wants' to be close to people.

He craves two things: food and affection. He longs for them and desires them passionately. I assume he even dreams about them. When his wants aren't fulfilled, he does weird things...like going potty on our nice, light-beige carpet or hiding in his kennel.

In the same way, your husband has a clear set of 'wants.' They are the things that he craves and desires almost as much as air and water. In fact, these wants are basically the same for every husband from Afghanistan to Zanzibar. And, when these 'wants' aren't met, he reacts.

If I were to discuss your 'wants', you'd know right away what I was talking about. Just for fun, let me ask you a couple of questions. What does every woman crave, desire, and want from a man? What did you want before you were married?

Actually, I already know the answers because you want(ed) what every woman wants...and it's what my eight-year-old daughter wants too, although she doesn't yet verbalize it.

My little Katherine wants a knight-in-shining armor who will treat her like a princess.

It's also what you wanted in a man before you were married. You wanted someone to treat you gently, slay dragons for you, get lost in your eyes, and spend hours talking soul to soul about life and how much he adores you.

You wanted a man who would cherish you and do anything for you...a knight-in-shining armor who would treat you like a princess.

Those were and still are your wants. You crave and desire them from your innermost being.

Your husband was *that man* before you were married. He opened car doors, talked to you for hours, traveled great distances without complaint just to be with you, treated you gently, adored you...and then married you.

Now he complains when he has to run to the store for you, talks in grunts, and treats you more like the dragon than the princess who needs rescuing.

Just as you have these God-given basic desires, needs and wants, so too, does your husband. So, let's talk about what every man, young and old alike, wants from a woman. Men aren't as complex as women. All they want is someone to help them, follow them, encourage them, believe in them, admire them, and desire them. A man wants someone to think his ideas are brilliant, his muscles strong, his jokes funny, and his ambitions noble. He wants someone to cling to him and snuggle deep into his rippling muscles.

Don't laugh! You used to do that for your husband before you were married.

That's what your husband craves and desires with intense passion. Know what he gets instead? Drip...drip...drip... drip...drip...a dripping faucet, constantly reminding him that he is not the spiritual leader, father, and husband that you wish he was.

You may be tempted to think that your husband doesn't feel this way, but you might be surprised.

Your husband may never tell you this but he knows he's not the leader you want him to be. He knows you'd like him to be more involved with the family. He knows you want him to be more communicative and spend less time on his things. Your husband knows all these things because you often remind him of how he's let you down. When you do this, he pulls further away from you.

When your husband doesn't get what he needs or wants, you don't get what you need or want. Nagging, shouting, and manipulating the situation certainly won't work. The only way to <u>see</u> changes in him is to <u>change</u> how you see him.

So, let's take a look at what every husband needs and how you as a wife can meet those needs. Your faithfulness will be rewarded by his involvement.

Let's Talk

1. In your opinion, what is the biggest difference in your marriage since you started homeschooling?

_____

2. If you were totally honest, how would you rate the health of your marriage as it is today on a scale of 1 (failing) to 10 (glorious)?

_____

3. Using the stem and the leaves analogy, list as many 'leaves' as you can think of in one minute.

_____

_____

4. Why do you think the leaves often become more important and time consuming in our lives than the stem?

_____

_____

5. Thinking of all your duties and responsibilities, how do you think your husband would rank his importance on that list?

_____

Why do you think that?

_____

_____

6. What were some of the things that first attracted you to your husband?

_____

_____

7. What were some of the things that first attracted him to you? This is no time to be modest.

_____

_____

8. The truth is that most wives come across as dripping faucets sometimes. What do you 'drip' most often about?

_____

9. How does your husband respond to the dripping?

_____

_____

UNTIL NEXT TIME
· ·

Listen to yourself this week and keep track of all the times you 'drip' on your husband. You can keep a mental score card, or better yet, make a small note in the space provided.

_____

_____

CHAPTER 2

Every Husband Wants A Helper

LET'S START AT the very beginning...with creation. Adam was perfect and sinless in every way, having an untainted relationship with his creator. He had it all...or at least it appears that way as you read the account in Genesis.

However, God looked at his perfect man and said, "It is not good for the man to be alone..." Stop.

If I had been there, I might have raised my hand and said, "Excuse me God, but he isn't alone. He has YOU. What more could he want or need? I mean, I beg your pardon, but we've been told by pastors and teachers that all we need is a relationship with YOU."

Had I said that, I would have been wrong because apparently God's man was not complete yet...there was still something missing.

God said, "It is not good for the man to be alone. I will make a helper suitable for him." And then God put Adam to sleep, and from a rib, he created a "suitable helper"—Eve.

The little phrase "suitable helper" packs a big punch, containing the primary reason for woman's creation and ultimately, her job description. The woman was created to be the man's 'helper.'

In our current society, that doesn't always settle real well with women. Somehow, the title 'helper' has become synonymous with 'inferior doormat.' It has become a despised label instead of a title of honor.

God says being a 'helper' is a good thing. He knew Adam needed someone to complete him. Adam could not accomplish what God had asked him to do alone; he needed someone else. If Adam had needed a fishing buddy and a bass boat to complete him, God would have provided those things, but he didn't.

God knew Adam needed a wife to help him become what he was created to be. In the same way, God knew your husband needed YOU to complete him, to help him become what God intends him to be.

That's a good thing...an incredibly difficult thing, but a good thing.

Helpers Help

I don't mean to belabor the obvious, but a helper is someone who...helps. And if a helper doesn't help...he or she isn't a helper. Helpers voluntarily set aside their own wants, desires, and ambitions to help another accomplish his wants desires, and ambitions.

That's not easy to do. It's hard to set our own desires aside to help someone else achieve his. But that's what your husband needs and wants from you. He doesn't want to demand it though; he wants you to lovingly set them aside for him.

Sitting before me is my favorite brown leather Bible. It was a gift from my wife during our first year of marriage. I love this Bible, not because its pages are worn and marked or because I know where certain verses and passages lie on the page, but because of the inscription on the inside page written by my wife.

> *My Dear Husband,*
> *May you always know that where you go I will go, and where you stay I will stay. Your people will be my people and your God my God. Where you die I will die, and there I will be buried. May the Lord deal with me, be it ever so severely, if anything but death separates you and me.*
> *I am forever committed to you Todd.*
> *Happy Birthday my love,*
> *Debbie*

Man, that kind of note gets my heart thumping. What it says to me is this: Todd I'll help you be whatever it is you want to be. I'll follow you come hell or high water. I'll stick to you like gum...through thick and thin, for better or worse...until the end. AMEN!

That's what men want from their wives. That's what your husband wants from you.

For Adam, it was easy. God told him to be a gardener. So Eve's job was to help him be a gardener. We don't know how she helped him, but I can imagine her bringing him a big glass of lemonade, praying for his strength, telling him how great the garden looked, and sometimes sitting nearby in the cool of the morning just to be with her man.

That's a helper.

So what does God want your husband to be...a plumber, contractor, engineer, teacher, salesman, or nuclear scientist? Let's not forget your husband's most important tasks as husband and father.

As strange as it might sound, you are to help your husband be a good husband and father.

He can't be a good husband and father without you. You're his helper remember? Now don't get too excited yet. I'm not talking about telling him how to do his job...that's nagging.

So how do you help your husband be what God created him to be?

It might be as simple as asking him how you can pray for his day at work. Every husband loves to know his wife cares about what he does while he is away from home. Most wives have communicated that they don't care what he does at work; they just want him to be involved when he gets home.

Another way you can help your husband is to help him be ready for work each day. Sounds easy, but when you make sure your husband's clothes are clean and ready to go, you help him be what he was created to be.

Maybe you think you don't have time to iron his shirts and there's no reason he can't take care of it himself.

He could, but then you miss out on the opportunity to show him that you want to help him. The same is true with making his lunch or packing his suitcase when he travels. I heard of one wife who was married to a professional golfer tell how she cleaned her husband's clubs the night before each important match.

Now that made her husband feel loved.

As a writer, my home office gets buried in mountains of paper and trash. Not too long ago, I left for the day on business. When I came home, I opened the door of my office to a spotlessly clean room. I gasped when I saw my uncluttered desk, clean floor, and all the books neatly stacked on the shelf.

Immediately, a wave of emotion hit me. It felt incredible to know my wife believed in me and was trying to help me be a writer.

That's what your husband wants. It may take a little creativity, but I bet you can come up with five different ways you can help your husband be what God has created him to be.

In the following chapters, I will give you practical direction in being your hubby's ultimate helper.

Let's Talk

1. If you asked your husband what he was created to be, what do you think he would say?

2. How would you rank yourself as his helper, 1 (not at all) to 10 (a wonderful helper)?

3. What sacrifices have you made to be his helper?

4. Would he say you are happily making those sacrifices?

5. List five things you can do to help your man.

6. How can you help your husband be a better husband without nagging? Think about this one.

_____

_____

7. How can you help your husband be a better father without nagging?

_____

_____

UNTIL NEXT TIME
. . . .

Say one positive comment to your husband each day for the next week or until your next group meeting.

CHAPTER 3

Every Husband Wants to be Followed

EVERY MAN WANTS someone who will follow him to the end of the world and back. In fact, one of the best ways you can 'help' your husband is by following him.

Don't let this idea make you feel inferior because it will keep you from following your husband. And when you don't follow, you significantly hinder him from becoming what God created him to be, which in turns affects the outcome of your homeschool.

Did you realize that in addition to being created to help your husband, you were also created to follow your husband? Let me illustrate the point:

A dog sled team is the perfect picture of our roles as husband and wife.

The concept is simple: a bunch of dogs pull a sled across the snow, guided by the master who stands on the tail end of the sled. The dogs aren't controlled by reins but by voice commands from the master (now if you happen to be into dog sledding please do not write me to tell me how little I know about dog sledding).

Here's the important part: every sled team has one dog in the front that is responsible for guiding the rest of the team. He is called...the lead dog. His job is to listen to the master, and do as he commands. When the master says, "Turn right," he turns right. When the master says, "Stop," he stops.

The lead dog isn't more important than the other dogs; he just has a specific role. All the dogs are loved, given the same reward, and expected to work hard.

Now imagine that a sled team is mushing along some frozen lake, when all of a sudden, the master cries out, "Turn right!" But instead of doing as he's told, the lead dog turns left.

The master pulls the team to a stop, steps from behind the sled, walks past the other dogs until he reaches the lead dog, and then smacks the dog on the head and says, "I said turn right." The lead dog takes the full brunt of the master's fury. After all, it was his job to listen and lead. The other happy dogs aren't punished because they were doing their job of following the lead dog.

Suppose though, that when the master called out, "Turn right," that instead of following the lead dog, the dog behind him tried to correct the lead and keep him from going the wrong way by turning right.

Guess who gets in trouble now?

Both. The lead dog for not listening to his instructions AND the other dog for not following the lead dog. Now, I'm not an animal rights activist, but doesn't that seem unfair? After all, why should the dog behind the lead dog get in trouble for doing what the master instructed?

The answer: because that dog's role was to <u>follow</u> the lead dog.

Your husband is the lead dog, and your role is to follow him.

Following Isn't Always Fun

Following is easy when your lead dog is going where you want to go, but it's a whole different story when your lead dog is leading you somewhere you don't want to go.

It's even worse when your lead dog doesn't seem to be listening to the master.

So what do you do?

You follow the lead dog anyway.

But what if your husband...I mean, lead dog is doing something stupid? Shouldn't you do what you can to make it right?

No. Your role is to follow the lead dog. In fact, God honors a wife who follows her lead dog...even when the lead dog is going the wrong direction. Besides, your husband will either love you for following him, or despise you for pushing him aside and taking over his job.

One more thing. Husbands know when you're following begrudgingly. When you say things like, "OK, I'll go, but I think it's a dumb move," you're not following. You're being dragged, and lead dogs know when the rest of the team is dragging behind.

They can see it in your face, in the tone of your voice, and in the way you talk to others. Your lead dog wants you to enjoy the ride, and brag about how smart and brave he is along the way.

Believe me, if you follow your husband joyfully, he will love you for it!

That is the essence of the note in my Bible, "Where you go, I will go, and where you stay, I will stay." My wife didn't just write it though; she has lived it.

Our Story

For over a decade I was a pastor. We loved the little church we were a part of, and our life was great. We had five children, a wonderful house, a great church family filled with friends, AND a weekly paycheck that covered the expenses of raising a family.

That was all threatened when I began to feel the tension of trying to be a writer, a pastor, a husband and a dad. I began to pray, " God, I can't do all this...what do you want me to do?"

My wife and I talked about the struggle for over a year, until one day, while lounging by the lake on vacation, my wife suggested, "Why don't we give it a try? You could quit, and we could really give this writing thing a shot."

I felt like I had been handed the world. We talked and prayed more, and six months later we announced that we were leaving the church and heading out on a new adventure. I was at the helm, and my wife was right behind me, helping me be what God had created me to be.

The next year was scary. There was no paycheck, no income, and no prospects on the horizon. Things were tight, and doubts plagued us...but hear this loud and clear...not once did my wife ever question my leading. She had every right to, and no one would have blamed her; but she never once said, "I can't believe I let you talk me into this stupid idea. Everything was so nice back there...now look at us."

Do you know how that makes a man feel? Incredible.

You may not believe this, but it's not always fun being the lead dog. There's a lot of pressure to make right decisions...and usually we make the wrong decision, but there is no greater feeling than knowing that our woman is right behind us all the way.

That's what every husband wants from his wife.

Bad Leading

But what if your husband is leading you into a bad situation financially? What if your husband is terrible with finances but gets defensive if you try to take the responsibility from him?

You put your arm around your man, hold tight, buckle your seatbelt and get ready for a wild ride on the financial rollercoaster.

Remember, finances are just the leaves of the plant. Your relationship with your husband is the STEM. You can recover from bankruptcy. You'll never fully recover if you lose your marriage.

Some men, however, will lead by deciding that their wives should handle the finances under their direction. You can discuss this option with your husband…you can talk about anything. Pick a non-confrontational time to talk (not right after the bank calls about a bad check). Tell your husband how you feel, and then ask if he would mind letting you do the finances (because he's busy and you like to do them). If your husband says yes, then you can help him without taking something away from him. But if he gets defensive, then back off and love your man, regardless of how wild the ride gets.

Lightbulbs

Trying to define whose role it is to do the finances, the banking, or taking out the trash is a delicate balance. Some of these roles are woven into the very fabric of who we are. For me, changing the lightbulbs in the house is one of them.

For some reason, God has placed the burden of responsibility deep within me to change lightbulbs. Unfortunately for my wife, I'm a procrastinator.

I used to work for a guy who was every woman's dream. If a lightbulb went out in the fixture above the kitchen table, he had it changed before the lightbulb cooled down. I'm the kind of guy who would let all the lightbulbs in the room burn out, and then I'd move to another room.

But, when I see my wife up on a chair changing a lightbulb, I feel defensive. Why? Because when she changes a lightbulb, it serves as a reminder that I've let her down and it sounds like dripping water to me. She may not intend for it to sound that way, but that's how I hear it.

My wife feels the same way when she finds me sewing a button on my favorite shirt that has sat near the end of the bed for a few months. She feels like she let me down. I tell her I know she's busy and I don't mind, but still it serves as a reminder that she is not being a good wife.

When you take out the trash because your husband forgot, make a car appointment with the garage because he's put it off for months, or take over doing the checkbook because he hasn't balanced it in years, you step out of your role as follower and take over the lead.

Even if the trash is piling up or the car is about to fall apart, unless your husband asks you to intervene or delegates the task, you mustn't rob him of his role by doing it yourself. A neglected task is a leaf; your relationship with your husband is the stem.

Why Some Men Don't Lead

Most men are afraid to lead and make decisions. You know why? Because their wives have told them they don't like their decisions. Take the age-old, 'where do you want to eat' scenario, for example. The husband asks his wife where she wants to eat. The wife says she doesn't care and tells him to decide. Then he suggests someplace, and she says she doesn't want to eat there. So he names another place, but she doesn't want to eat there either.

Finally, the frustrated husband tells her to pick where she wants to eat, but without batting an eye, she says she wants him to decide.

Sound familiar? Let me give you a peek into the head of that husband. Deep inside he's thinking, *why does she ask me? She doesn't want my opinion; she just wants to do what she wants to do.* The next time his wife asks his opinion, he won't give it because he knows she won't listen to it. I know because I'm one of those guys.

The story I'm about to share is true...although my wife will deny it.

When we were first married and getting ready for church one day, my wife asked, "Which socks do you like better—the ones on the right or the ones on the left?"

Without thinking I answered, "What's it matter...no one's going to be looking at your socks." Wrong answer. Next time would be different.

A couple of months later, when my wife asked again, "Which socks do you like better—the ones on the right or the ones on the left?" I quickly responded, "The ones on the right."

She said, "But you didn't even think about it."

So I said, "Who cares...no one's going to be looking at your socks." Wrong answer.

Now when she comes up to me and asks the same question, I think for a few minutes and then respond, "The ones on the right."

Then my wife wears the ones on the LEFT instead. Everyone knows that typically when a woman asks a question, and a man gives his opinion, the woman does the opposite.

That's why men don't lead or give their input. Because when they do, their wives say, "No, not like that!"

So when your husband leads even in the smallest matter—let him. If he chooses your least favorite restaurant in the world, you'd be wise to say, "That sounds great." If you encourage him when he leads a little, he'll lead a little more the next time.

Maybe you're among the millions of wives who say, "Yeah, but my husband doesn't lead—ever. What about me? What am I supposed to do?"

The Passive Husband

A passive male takes a passive, hands-off approach to life. I've known men like this. You can ask them to tell you the color of the sky, and they won't give you a straight answer.

"That's a good question," they'll say, hoping to avoid a real answer.

After asking for her husband's input
for 3 years, Jim finally offered his opinion
for the **first** and **last** time.

Maybe you're married to a passive male. You didn't mind it when you were dating, because he was always deferring to you..."Let's eat where you want to eat...I'll do whatever you'd like...Sure I like those kind of movies...you're right, I was wrong."

Now that you're married, you desperately want him to have an opinion on something. What used to seem like caring now comes across as spineless passivity.

Passive men usually aren't born that way. More often than not, they've been encouraged to be that way by one of two people: their mother or their wife. Let's consider the mother first.

You've seen the child who can never seem to please his mother. She's constantly telling him, "Not that way...no, like this...never mind, I'll do it." He tries to please her but is never able to. After a while, the child quits trying. It's safer to be quiet and lay low than to stick his neck out where it will just get chopped off.

When the child becomes a husband, he'll continue to lay low and be quiet, afraid to take a stand or become involved for fear of failing. If this describes your husband, then you need to allow your husband to lead safely.

First, get out of the driver's seat and force him to lead. If something is his job, then let him do it. If it doesn't get done, then let it not get done. If you allow him, he'll let you lead forever. If you refuse to lead, eventually he'll have to lead.

When he finally takes his first little run as the lead dog, follow him. Even if you think it's not the best idea or the right

40

direction, let him experience the joy of leading and being followed by his woman.

<u>Praise him</u> when he helps with the kids, takes out the trash, or listens to you rant about a day of homeschooling. Don't correct him when he disciplines a child, or bark at him for getting lost on the way to Aunt Edna's. Don't criticize or nag, because he'll withdraw and shrink back.

Praise him for any involvement he gives. Follow his lead, and he will lead more. When you do that, you give your husband a great gift: you help him be a better husband and father.

Sometimes a man has been "trained" to be passive by his wife...his nagging wife. The man came into the marriage ready to lead, but over time he found that it was safer to keep his opinions to himself and became convinced that his wife knows better.

This husband is like a dog that has had his nose slapped so many times that he flinches every time someone lifts a hand. He has learned that at home it's easier and safer to stay in the shadows. At the office he may lead up a storm, but at home he blends into the woodwork because it's "her" turf.

Maybe you're wondering if you've been the cause of your husband's passivity. Have you heard any of these phrases tumble out of your mouth?

"I should have done it myself."

"You always do it wrong."

"Can't you do anything right?"

"That's a dumb idea."

"I told you to..."

If these words ring a bell, then you have caused your husband to believe that his place in the family is as dad the figurehead. He has the title but no real authority...that's yours. But underneath all that, he still longs for you to follow him and to hear from you that he's doing a good job.

So here's what you do: quit leading. Refuse to lead in your husband's place, forcing him to step up to the plate. When he does lead at whatever level, follow your lead dog. Tell him he was great, smart, wise, and strong...and any other adjectives you can think of. Thank him for leading and then wait for him to do it again.

1. Would your husband say he's the lead dog in your family?

2. In what area is it difficult for you to allow your husband to lead?

3. Does leading come easily for your husband? Why or why not?

4. How could you encourage him to lead?

_____

_____

5. How do you discourage him from leading?

_____

_____

6. How could God use your husband's leading (right or wrong) to change you?

_____

_____

UNTIL NEXT TIME
· ·

Make this your prayer for the next week: *"God, help me to allow my husband to lead, especially in the area I listed in question #2. Teach me to follow no matter where he goes."*

CHAPTER 4

Every Husband Wants an Encourager

WHAT IS ENCOURAGEMENT exactly? Webster defines it as: to inspire with courage, to support. Encouragement is NOT telling your husband <u>to be</u> more involved in family, communication, and homeschooling. It is inspiring and supporting your husband <u>in what</u> he was created to be.

One comes across as nagging...the other as cheering.

One builds walls...the other opens doors.

One wants...the other gives.

One is a reminder of failure...the other is a reminder of how much they are loved.

One of the greatest examples of encouragement I ever witnessed happened about 10 years ago during the summer Olympic games. It involved the women's gymnastic team when they were going for the gold. It was down to the last event—the vault.

A diminutive Kerri Strug stepped up to the line, ran the length of the runway, vaulted into the air, and then landed in a crumpled heap on the mat crying in pain. She had hurt her ankle. Kerri was out, and the Americans had lost...at least that's what everyone thought. A deafening cheer erupted ten minutes later, when Kerri hobbled to the line with a heavily bandaged ankle and tears in her eyes.

The crowd stared in disbelief. How could she endure the pain of another run, let alone the landing? It was insane.

Or was it? The camera panned to the sideline and focused on her coach. He had a bushy mustache and stood with his arms folded. Suddenly, he clapped his hands and shouted, "You can do it, Kerri! You can do it!" He shouted this over and over.

You know what? She did it, and America won the gold.

This is the kind of encouragement your husband needs. He wants a cheerleader wife standing on the sideline...or better yet, clinging to his arm, cheering, "You can do it, Honey! You can do it!"

He wants you to encourage him in whatever he chooses to do.

What if you're married to a work-a-holic who spends 70 hours a week at the office and another 20 hours a week working at home answering emails and working on the computer?

Surely I'm not asking you to encourage your husband in that.

That's exactly what I'm saying.

Thank him for working so hard for your family. Kiss him with a steel-melting kiss before he heads off to work in the morning. Slap him on the tush and say, "Go get 'em Tiger."

If he spends too much time on hobbies over the weekend, don't nag him or guilt him into spending time with the family...it won't work anyway. Instead, cheer him on and tell him that you hope he wins the round of golf or catches the biggest fish. I'm telling you, your husband will love you for that.

"Yeah, but how will that get him more involved in family?" you ask.

It will. Trust me on this one. The more he feels loved and encouraged in what he does and who he is, the more he'll want to be with you. The opposite is just as true. If he feels like a failure at home and a loser of a husband and father, he won't want to be around home, the children, or you.

Not only should you encourage your husband in his work and hobbies, but you should also encourage him in family and marriage. Instead of saying, "You never spend any time with your children...they're going to grow up and hate you...", look for the times, be they ever so small, when he has done something with the kids and praise him.

If he makes a point to be home for dinner one night, tell him how much you enjoyed having him there and how much the kids enjoyed it, too. Don't add that you'd like to challenge him to be home every night...just thank him for what he did do.

If he offers to help you do the dishes, clear off the table, or whatever...let him. Don't tell him he's doing it wrong or ask for more. Just say, "Thank you."

I talked to one woman who said that she told her husband that she was "turned on" (sorry all you Baptists) when she watched her husband vacuum. That man probably wore out the carpet from vacuuming after his wife said that.

You can do the same. It's not tricking your husband into

getting what you want; it's loving him, as you would like to be loved.

Here are some other ways you can encourage your husband:

* Thank him for going to work.
* Tell him you're praying for his big meeting, deadline, or other event.
* Tuck a small note in his pocket or set it on the seat of his car telling him how proud you are of him.
* If he comes home and said he had a good game of golf, ahhh and oooo about it. Take him on a date to celebrate.
* Email him at work telling him how much you appreciate the income he provides for your family.
* Thank him for a great vacation, or a nice home or car.
* After a time of intimacy, thank him for being a great lover.
* If he does something helpful around the house, thank him with a hug.

Your husband may wonder what's come over you or what the catch is, but prove to him that your only motive is to love him as God would have you love him.

Do you feel overwhelmed already? Does this sound like a lot of work? Are you wondering how you're supposed to do all that you do AND write notes, send emails, and pat tushes?"

It's a choice. You need to decide whether you want to spend your time and energy on the leaves or the stem.

Read this letter on the following page from a wife who chose to put her husband first.

Dear Todd,

I ordered the last session on tape "for women only" from the homeschool convention. It was really good. I'm sure I've heard it all before. But I believe when God speaks to us, we don't hear what he has for us until we're ready to listen.

Also through different stages in our lives, we must need different advice toward our husbands. I mean it's all the same, but we aren't the same. We change. We go through spurts where everything's great between spouses. Then things happen— lots of things, and we don't even realize it, but this is when we really need these words of wisdom from God to remind us of how to get back to where we should be in relationship to our husbands. I must have been in one of my "need a reminder" spurts.

Last night, we were supposed to have a date night. I was out grocery shopping and my husband and I were supposed to meet back home to go on our date at 5 pm. Well, the weather was pretty scary. I was passing cars in ditches everywhere. So I was really concentrating on driving.

My husband called and said, "Hey, I'm not going to be able to make it by 5:00. I didn't get everything done I needed to and have to finish before I come home. Can you just meet me back here in town?" That really didn't settle well, while driving in the snowy weather. Note: I was listening to your tape at that very time he called. I had this agenda in mind and he was going to wreck it. I told him I was in the middle of this awful driving weather and really looking forward to not driving again. He said that maybe we shouldn't go to the mall if the weather was so bad. What he was really saying was that he didn't want to spend our date night shopping. So I proceeded to explain to him why it was so important for us to go to the mall. Then he said that I didn't really care about the date, just the tasks I needed to accomplish.

Well, I decided to think through what to do for the rest of my intense drive home and told him I'd call him back when I had a clear mind. Of course it was your voice, Todd, coming out "preaching" to me the whole way home. So by the time I got home, I knew what to do. I called him back up and said, "Hey, why don't we just stay in town and go to a movie and dinner afterward. I'll just wait here until you get home and then we'll go." I could hear him smile!! All this to say, we had an awesome date night. I believe it was all because I made the right decision to make our night a date night and not an agenda to use our date night to accomplish my list!

While we were eating, my husband leaned in toward me and said, "So what's going on with you? You seem different." He gave me several examples, which I was shocked that he noticed such petty things. I realized right then that I was letting God work in me to make changes without even realizing that changes were happening. It was awesome. I felt like a million bucks! And I'm sure he was feeling the same. So I plan to pop that tape in my tape deck every time I start getting into one of my lousy ruts as a reminder of where I want to be in relation to my husband.

Thanks for encouraging!
A wife in Indiana

Let's Talk

1. Name three people that you would consider "encouragers." What do they say or do that makes you feel encouraged?

_____

_____

_____

2. How would you rank yourself on the "encourager" scale? 1 (being a discourager) to 10 (being a super encourager).

_____

3. What do you sometimes do that discourages your husband?

_____

_____

What really encourages him?

_____

_____

4. What hinders you from being the kind of encourager you know your husband needs you to be?

_____

_____

UNTIL NEXT TIME
. . . .

The best time to prepare for a fire is before you have one...the best time to plan to encourage your husband is right now. List 3 ways you can encourage your husband in the coming week, then do it.

1. _____

2. _____

3. _____

CHAPTER 5

Every Husband Wants to be Believed In

WE'VE TALKED ABOUT helping, following and encouraging. These all seem doable if you believe in your husband's direction, but what if you don't believe your husband is going where God wants him to go? Suppose he's about to pack up the family, move to the other side of the country, and start a Chinchilla farm? What then?

Believe in HIM, even if you don't believe in the direction he's going. AND, believe that God will honor you for believing in your husband.

Really, as husbands, we just want our wives to believe in us. We want you to believe that we're capable, smart, and strong and brave enough to see the family through. More often than not, you remind us that we're incapable, stupid, and weak.

Guess how warm and fuzzy that makes us feel towards you?

But when you believe in us, we are drawn toward you and towards being more involved, especially in the three important areas that I'm about to discuss.

Discipline

I know you want your husband to be active in the discipline of your children. All wives do. The way to get him more involved is to believe in him.

Oftentimes what happens is a husband overreacts, starts yelling, doles out some oversized punishment, and then his wife jumps into action undoing all that he has done.

"You're being too hard on him...It wasn't all his fault...I think that was very unfair of you..." she might say.

When a wife does that, he mentally decides not to get involved in disciplining his children anymore. So he doesn't. And then his wife complains that he never helps with the discipline. See the problem?

In order to get your husband involved in disciplining your children, you must believe in him when he does discipline. Even if he yells too loud or doles out an oversized punishment, believe that God is able to use your husband's wrong reactions to accomplish what He wants accomplished.

Instead of correcting your husband, tell him that you sure appreciate his help. I promise that your husband will be more involved in disciplining your children if you do that consistently.

This doesn't mean you can never talk about how he might have overreacted, just don't do it right then in the heat of it. Pick a non-confrontational time when the kids aren't around.

Warning: if your husband is not very involved, I would be hesitant about telling him even in a non-confrontational time. He may feel threatened and pull himself out of the game.

Family Devotions

The same holds true in the area of family devotions. Women have been duped into thinking that 'real' godly families have family devotions, and in order to be a REAL godly family, your husband needs to lead your family in devotions.

The way to assure that your husband will never lead family devotions is it to nag him about it or give him a book on how REAL godly families do it. That just serves as a reminder that he's letting you down...and he already knows that.

Here's what I'd do. Wait until he makes the first move. Somewhere along the pike, he'll be encouraged by me or someone else to give family devotions a try.

When he does, praise your husband for doing it no matter how different it looks from what you were expecting. Chances are, he'll call the family together, read the Christmas story (in July), sing a chorus of Jingle Bells (in July), yell at the kids (in July), send one to his room, and pray a sentence prayer.

Don't say, "That wasn't very spiritual. Elizabeth Elliot's father sang hymns...and brought out deep Biblical truths." That would just reinforce what he already believes...and that is he is incapable of leading his family.

So what should you say instead?

"Honey, that was good...I was moved." OK maybe not that much sap, but you get the idea. Thank him for taking the time and for making it happen. Communicate that you believe in him. He will respond to that and will try it again.

Communication

While we're at it, let's tackle the last of the big 3—communication (discipline, devotions, & communication). When I say the word communication, you and your husband have two totally different definitions in mind.

To your husband, communication means to talk...you know, "How was your day, dear? That's fine. I'll be in the bathroom until dinner."

For you, communication means more...a lot more. You want eye-to-eye, soul-to-soul communication where you sit on the couch and talk for hours about life, spiritual issues, and how to have a better marriage and family.

So how do you believe in your husband in the area of communication? You encourage him when he talks to you at any level. When he sits on the couch and talks about his day but forgets to ask about yours, be satisfied. Tell him you loved hearing about his day, and he may give you a little more the next time. Talking about light, non-important things will pave the way for deeper conversations...the soul-to-soul kind that you crave so badly.

You will never improve your husband's communication skills by reminding him that he's not doing a very good job. (He probably already knows that anyway). When you say, "You never talk to me about important things...you just exchange facts...I want you to talk to me about how you feel," he'll draw further away. Instead, nourish the stem and the leaves of communication will grow.

Just Like Dear Old Mom

Once when I was sharing this concept with a huge group of women, a lady in the back yelled out and said, "It sounds like our husbands want their mother not a wife." All the ladies laughed, but the more I thought about it, the more I had to agree with her. It's not that a man wants his wife to treat him like a child, but he does want the same kind of encouragement that a mother gives a child.

You show this kind of love every day to your children. They walk up to you excited about something special behind their back and beam a big smile. Then they whip out a drawing of smeared crayon and pencil and exclaim, "Look at what I made Mom!"

"Wow," you say, "that looks really good. You are such a good artist...you are such a good boy. Let's put that on the refrigerator right now."

Actually, even as I type this, my son, Abraham, has just spent the last 10 minutes creating a mouse pad for my computer mouse. You should see his face and the sparkle in his smile. He even taped it under my mouse just for me.

When he said, "Do you like it?" I didn't say, "No. It won't work...why would you think you could make a mouse pad out of folded up paper? Besides it's too slippery...the ball on the bottom won't move on that. Just take it off and throw it in the trash."

Of course I didn't say that, I'm a dad.

Instead, I said what you would have said, "Thank you

so much, Abe. That's really nice. I love you so much. Thanks for making that for me."

THAT'S WHAT YOUR HUSBAND WANTS AND NEEDS FROM YOU!

So why is it that usually when your husband comes to you with some great idea, his eyes sparkling, that as soon as the words are out of his mouth, he knows you're not pleased?

Instantly, you rain on his parade, and his sparkle vanishes. He feels embarrassed and stupid. He may even temporarily— hate you for popping his bubble. That's the power you have over your husband.

Instead of lamenting the fact that he wants you to be like his mother, why not use some of the same skills that you use as a mother to show your husband you believe in him?

Let's Talk

1. When is it hardest to believe in your husband?

_____

_____

2. How do your show your "unbelief" in him?

_____

_____

3. From your perspective, how could God use your husband's "goofy" ideas to get you where HE wants YOU to be and be what HE wants YOU to be?

_____

_____

4. Name one area in which you're having trouble "believing" in your husband right now.

_____

5. How can you help other homeschooling moms believe in their husbands?

_____

UNTIL NEXT TIME

Make a conscious effort to use some of the love you use as a mother on your husband this week.

CHAPTER 6

Every Husband Wants to be Admired

IMAGINE YOU'RE SITTING across the table from your boyfriend at a favorite hangout. It's warm, and the room is festive and alive. People are talking around you, but you can't hear them. Your full attention is focused on the man sitting across from you.

Actually, you're not even sure what he's talking about, but you hang on every word. Your eyes sparkle and your smile assures him that you're enjoying the time. You stay and talk late into the night, and then he walks you home and kisses you at the front door.

The next day all you can talk about with your friend is the time you had with your guy. "He is so smart...and he's so funny and thoughtful...and he wants to own his own business," you tell her dreamily.

That's what it means to admire your husband. In case you didn't know it, the above illustration reflects how you used to feel toward your husband. Remember him...the guy you used to admire? He loved it then, and he longs for you to admire him now.

The problem is, now you're more likely to insult your husband than to talk about how great he is. I've heard wives and husbands snub their mates in front of the other...in fact, I've done it myself.

It sounds something like this:

* "You mean your husband restored that car himself? Bob can't even change the oil on our car."
* "Mike brought you flowers!?" Did you hear that, Honey? Her husband brought her flowers because he loves her. Bob's idea of romance is new filters for the furnace."
* "I love your new house. I've told Bob that if he ever makes some real money, this is the kind of place I'd love to get."

When these kinds of jabs are given, people might laugh, and maybe even the spouse will laugh at himself, but the spouse has been wounded. Like I said, I've caused these wounds to my wife, and I hate it.

Maybe you've gotten into the habit of taking little jabs at your husband. You might think they're harmless, but over time they pile up with devastating results.

Instead, as your husband's helper, follower, and encourager, admire your husband in public (and in private) with phrases like:

* "My husband is so smart. It took a while, but he figured out the problem."
* "Honey, I think you're great, and I'm so blessed to have you as my husband."
* "Whoa, talk about looking like a stud. You still got it!"

* "You know I think you're doing a great job as a dad. I can tell you've been working at it."
* "You really made me feel loved the other day."

You tell me what man, woman, or child wouldn't respond to that kind of admiration. And if you sprinkle your conversation with phrases like that, your husband will be more involved in family, in your marriage, and in home educating your children.

I know because, it works on me. Not long ago, I pulled in the driveway and saw my wife standing by the side door. I assumed someone was hurt or bleeding, and that I was needed to rush someone to the emergency room.

"What's up?" I asked as I stepped from the car.

She didn't answer but walked up to me and threw her arms around my neck and gave me a huge love-filled hug and said, "I think you're great."

Man she had me wrapped around her little finger. I would have done anything for her right then— including cleaning out that nasty place under the refrigerator. She was admiring me, and I was basking in it.

Yes, it takes some planning and may not come naturally. You may have to be really creative to think how you can admire your husband. It might involve sitting down and remembering all the things you used to like about your husband.

But let me remind you—lack of admiration will damage the stem.

Before reading on, list seven things you admire about your husband.

_____

_____

_____

_____

_____

_____

_____

Say Cheese

One last thing. Do you smile very often? You know that thing you do when the edges of your mouth curl up. Admiration produces smiles. You used to smile at your husband all the time across a room, in a group of people, or when he spoke. Now your husband is more likely to fall over dead if you smile in his direction.

The power of a smile is amazing. A smile conveys that you like the one you're smiling at and are happy with him. I know that when I'm smiling, my children feel like everything is right with the world. But if I look at them with a scowl, they know dad is not pleased with them.

I was in the garage not long ago when suddenly I heard a crash. I turned to see a guilty boy who had turned to face me. He quickly searched my face to see what his chances of survival were. Then I surprised him and smiled, and he smiled back, feeling loved and loving me.

When is the last time you smiled at your husband even though he messed up, took the wrong road, or made a financial blunder? Try it tonight when he gets home from work. Greet him with a kiss and a smile. As he talks at the table—smile. When he tells you about something at work—smile. If he gets snappy at the children—smile.

If you're too tired after a day of homeschooling to smile, then rest or take a nap. If you can't get it all in and still smile...then don't get it all in. Think—stem. Adore your husband with smiles of admiration...because if YOU smile more, HE will be more involved in your family and in your life.

So, when in doubt—SMILE.

Let's Talk

1. When you were dating your husband, what traits did you most admire about him? List them:

_____

_____

_____

2. How did you show your admiration? How did he respond?

_____

_____

3. Would your husband say you admire him now? What do you think makes him feel that way?

_____

_____

UNTIL NEXT TIME

Brainstorm alone or with the group and come up with 10 things that you could say or do to show your husband that you admire him. Plan to say or do at least one of them this week. Write down his response to share with the group next time.

CHAPTER 7

Every Husband Wants to be Desired

THIS IS THE chapter you've been dreading. This is a difficult chapter for me to write because when I was growing up, my family didn't talk about such things. I knew everyone wore underwear at my house, we just never mentioned it.

Yet, this is such an important topic that it <u>must</u> be addressed. Your husband wants someone to desire him...and that someone is YOU.

I know you think I'm referring to SEX, but it's so much more than that. Desire is sexual, but it is also fun and flirtatious, spontaneous and wild. You know what I'm talking about because you used to desire your husband like this...when he wasn't your husband.

Now you're a homeschooling mom, and homeschooling moms aren't flirtatious or wild. When you walk down the mall and pass Victoria's Secret, and your husband nudges you towards the door, you say, "Are you kidding?!! I'm not going in there!"

When you say things like that, you confirm the fact in your husband's mind that you no longer desire him, and he pulls away. When he touches you and you pull away or bat him away, he withdraws from you and homeschooling.

He wants you to want him...I mean really WANT him.

Amish in Black

One winter day a few years ago, I was at the mall with my family. We were strolling along minding our own business when I noticed five or six Amish women walking in a line from tallest to shortest.

They were dressed in black from head to toe, all scurrying in the same direction. None of them carried any packages or bags except the last Amish woman. I wish I had my camera because the last woman held at her side a pink and white striped bag—Victoria's Secret.

Ker-ching! I wanted to give the woman a thumbs up signal and shout, "Way to go Amish lady! You're desiring your husband."

Now you may be thinking...*that's fine and dandy for the Amish lady, but I don't desire my husband—at all!*

Take heart, you're not alone.

I'd Rather Clean Toilets

After speaking to several hundred women in Ohio one year, a woman contacted me and said, "I was at the point that I'd rather clean toilets than be intimate with my husband." As we talked, it was verified that most wives have felt the very same thing at one time or another.

This wife attributed the lack of desire for her husband to a thyroid problem. After a lot of research and a variety of natural treatments, she began to desire her husband again.

As we talked, she suggested three reasons why a woman might no longer desire her husband.

The first reason, as I already mentioned, is hormonal. Now, I'm not a hormone or thyroid expert (I'm not quite sure what a thyroid does) so I won't pretend to give you any advice other than this: contact a doctor or friend whom you trust and see what you can do to remedy the situation.

Talk to your husband. Explain to him that you're going to get some help so you can once again desire him. If you take these measures, you will prove to your man that you care enough to get "fixed" for him, and he will feel desired and loved.

A second reason for lack of desire may be due to bitterness that you're holding on to. It could be bitterness against your husband or someone else, but it too will kill your desire for intimacy.

Again, you will need to talk to your husband and especially to God and deal with any unresolved bitterness. With your husband's blessing, you might want to make an appointment with a pastor or a counselor.

The last and most common reason for lack of desire is fatigue. You're just plain tired...you are a homeschooling mom, after all.

I know this is true for my wife. I'm the romantic in my marriage. After a long, hard day of homeschooling, and after getting the kids into bed, I'm the type of husband who would slip into our bedroom, light a few candles, and slip on a romantic CD.

One time my wife walked into this exact scenario, looked at the candles and said, "You've got to be kidding."

I wasn't kidding, and I slipped downstairs to pout.

Now if I were writing to husbands, I'd tell them to stop taking their wife's lack of desire personally and accept the fact that their just tired. I'd say, live with them in an understanding way. But to you, I say, if you ever walk into a room with candles lit, a black lacy thing sitting on the bed, and a romantic CD playing, smile and say, "I was thinking the same thing."

If you just feel too exhausted to desire any intimate time with your husband, then you need to get some rest.

Don't tell me it can't be done.

One word—STEM.

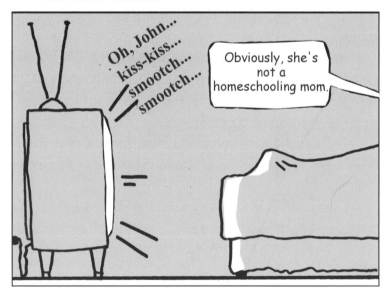

More Than Sex

Please don't misunderstand me and think I'm saying that desire is always synonymous with sex. It also includes the way you look at your husband, talk to him, and touch him.

I love it when my wife and I are lying in bed and she reaches out and gently strokes my arm or lays her head on my chest. I love it when she walks by me as I'm sitting at the computer and runs her hand across my shoulder...just to touch me. I love it when my wife looks at me and says, "Boy, you look good in that shirt," or "Have you been lifting weights? Your muscles feel bigger."

It gets my motor revving...and sometimes that's the problem.

My wife is AFRAID to touch me innocently because she's sure I'll take it as some kind of non-verbal cue that she's wanting more. I know it too. I know that she holds back just so I don't get the idea that she wants it to lead to something else.

Go out on a limb. You can touch, kiss, and smile, hoping that it will go no further, but don't withhold to assure that it won't.

Love freely and your husband will feel desired.

OK. Enough said about desire, except to say that this is also one of the keys to a successful homeschool and to getting your husband more involved in your family.

Let's Talk

1. Discuss the difference between your husband wanting SEX and wanting to be DESIRED.

2. List the obstacles that get in the way of desiring your husband.

3. Realistically, what would your husband require to feel like you desire him? Don't say, "He just wants IT every night." (That's probably an exaggeration and not totally true.)

4. What little things can you do to make your husband feel more desired?

5. How do you need to reorder your priorities to be able to desire your husband?

_____

_____

UNTIL NEXT TIME
· ·

List three things you need a friend to hold you accountable in to help you show your husband that you desire him. Now, go ask your friend to do so.

1. _____

2. _____

3. _____

CHAPTER 8

Every Husband Wants Acceptance

IN THE 70'S there was a popular song called, "I Love You Just the Way You Are." It was a hit probably because it embodied everyone's desire to be loved unconditionally.

That's what every husband wants from his wife. Unfortunately, the opposite is just as true. Most women say, "I'd love my husband more if he...

...spent more time with our family."

...communicated more."

...met some of my needs."

...acted like he cared about the kids."

...was more involved in homeschooling our children."

...lead family devotions."

...treated me better."

...spent less time at work."

...would give up his hobbies."

...or a hundred other things."

You know what? Your husband knows that you want him to be a better leader, and communicate more with you, and spend less time at work and more time with the family.

What he wants from you is what I've wanted from my wife at times and that is to be loved...really loved, just the way I am right now, not for what she'd like me to be in the future.

That's what your husband wants from you, too. By the way, you can't fake it. You can't act one way and pray another. Don't pray, "Lord, please change HIS heart. Make HIM see the wickedness of HIS ways...so that he'll give up seeking the unimportant and earnestly seek that which is best."

Instead pray, *"God, change ME. Help me to love my husband just the way he is, not for what he might become. Help me to be satisfied with Him as he is now. Let me encourage him, desire him, help and follow him right now. I may not believe in his dream, but help me to believe in HIM and to believe YOU."*

I truly believe that if you love your husband just the way he is (even if he never changes), he WILL become more involved in your family, in your marriage, and in homeschooling.

Let's Talk

1. Do you see how important it is to accept your husband just the way he is, even if he never changes?

2. Are you willing to love him unconditionally, the way God loves you?

---

3. Don't write these down, but make a mental list of all the areas in which your husband has let you down.

UNTIL NEXT TIME
· ·

Now, pray this prayer every day for the next week: *"God, change ME. Help me to love my husband just the way he is, not for what he might become. Help me to be satisfied with Him as he is now. Let me encourage him, desire him, help and follow him right now. I may not believe in his dream, but help me to believe in HIM and to believe YOU."*

CHAPTER 9

Every Husband Wants to Be #1

I WAS TALKING to a homeschooling mother just a couple of days ago. She was one of those meek and quiet mothers who ooze spiritualness. Besides looking the part, she had a bunch of children...that is, if you call 13 a bunch of children. From all outward appearances, she was the picture of ultimate homeschooling success.

As she talked to me, I realized there was a sad story under all the outward appearances. "Several years ago," she said, "my husband and I were on the verge of divorce. He was finished with our marriage and our family. We had drifted worlds apart and although we lived in the same house, we only existed together."

She told me her story of how God graciously and miraculously healed their marriage but it had been hard. I suspected he had gotten involved with someone else...or gotten into some bad stuff on the INTERNET, but she corrected my misconception.

"It all happened because he felt like I had put our children and homeschooling ahead of him...and he wanted to be #1," she said.

She stated what every husband wants from his wife...to be #1. That is why this book is entitled How to be a Great Wife...Even Though You Homeschool, because keeping your husband in 1st place is so hard...especially when you homeschool.

There is so much to do and accomplish. There are children to teach and care for, a house to keep clean, and clothes that need washed.

It's easy to take your husband for granted, to assume that he's OK and understands the importance of your job. It's not that you don't love and care about him...it's just that the squeaky wheel gets the oil, and he just doesn't squeak much (the kids squeak continually).

The result is that when a husband feels like he is way down the scale of importance, he gravitates towards the things that make him feel important...like work, hobbies, friends, or...someone else.

Is your heart sinking into your stomach? Do you feel a wave of defeat about to crash over you? NO!!! I'm not writing this to make you feel guilty; I'm writing to remind you which is the stem and which are the leaves.

You can't do it all, so don't even try. Take care of the stem, and the plant will thrive. If you make your husband feel like #1, your homeschool will be successful and your children will grow up ready and prepared for life.

Can it really be that simple? Yes!

Every Husband Feels Love Differently

I've discussed several things that all husbands want from their wives. The only thing left to mention is that one special "thing" that your husband needs from you to feel loved, helped, encouraged, and followed.

Husbands are like people...no two are alike. Each one has specific likes and dislikes. What makes one husband feel loved, leaves another hubby feeling...nothing.

You probably already know what really makes your husband feel loved, but if you don't...you need to ask him.

My sister-in-law asked this question of my youngest brother Dru. She had been attending a woman's Bible study that challenged the ladies to ask their husbands what they could do to make them feel more loved.

"Dru, how can I make you feel more loved?" My sister-in-law asked timidly.

Without much thought, my brother answered, "Don't make soup."

"What do you mean?"

"I don't like soup. You always make soup. My family didn't eat a lot of soup, and I don't like soup. So, don't make soup."

That's my brother.

You should be so lucky.

As I shared my sister-in-law's example with a large group of women once, one wife raised her hand and said, "I know what my husband needs from me to feel loved. All he needs is SEX!"

By the look on her face, I could tell she would have much preferred a "don't make soup" kind of husband. I reminded her of three things 1) Her husband wants more than sex. He wants her to want sex with him. 2) This is a stem issue. 3) If her husband needs SEX from her to feel loved, helped, followed, and encouraged, then she's faced with a choice. She can either change to make her husband feel loved, or she can continue on with business as usual. My sister-in-law faced the same choice regarding soup, and you are faced with the same choice regarding what makes your husband feel loved.

You probably have a dozen reasonable explanations for not doing everything you can to make your husband feel loved and helped. The lady above could have said (and rightly so), "It's not reasonable to have sex every day. No one else does that. I've got a life...and I'm tired...I've got a family to take care of...you're being unreasonable...and I'm not doing it."

My sister-in-law could have told my brother, "People eat soup, Dru. I like soup...other people serve their husbands soup...I'm going to make soup!"

To my sister in-law I'd say, "If all your husband needs to feel loved is for you to serve him solid food, you'd have to be dumb to serve him soup."

To the lady whose husband wants sex every night, I'd say the same. Yes, it's more difficult and involves more energy than going without soup, but if that's what your husband needs from you...do whatever you can to meet those needs.

I'll say the same to you. Whatever your husband needs from you to feel loved, do everything in your power to meet that need. If you have to take naps...take naps, if you have to take a correspondence course on the basics of football, take the course. If you have to learn how to fly fish...learn to fly fish. If you have to find a baby-sitter so you can go out once a week on a date with your husband...find a baby-sitter.

Whatever it is...do it.

Your husband is the stem, and if you meet his needs, he will become more involved in homeschooling, family, and your marriage.

If your husband doesn't feel loved, helped, followed...and all those other things, he will pull out of family, homeschooling, and your marriage.

It's hard to believe that homeschooling and how you treat your husband are related, but they are. When you were dating, you listened to his big ideas, believed in him, and offered to help him achieve his dreams...and he loved you for it. He in turn communicated with you in a deep way and treated you like a princess.

But now, you remind him that he's let you down, and you've become the dripping faucet that Proverbs 27:17 describes.

But there's hope! In fact, it's simpler than you might think.

Let's Talk

1. If your husband were to rank his importance in your life, where would he rank himself...1 (being the most important) to 10 (being the least important)?

_____

2. List the things you think HE would say are more important to you than him.

_____

_____

3. List the things you have let become more important than meeting your husband's needs.

_____

_____

4. Where does homeschooling rank in your list of importance? Has homeschooling replaced your husband as #1?

_____

5. What can you to do to make him feel #1? Write down the steps you need to take to accomplish that.

_____

_____

6. What is that one special thing (p. 67) your husband needs from you to feel loved, helped, encouraged, and followed?

_____

UNTIL NEXT TIME
· ·

Form your answer to question #5 into an accountability statement. Please hold me accountable to _____ in order to make my husband feel like he's number one in my life. Now, tell your friend to ask you next week how you're doing at this.

CHAPTER 10

Every Husband Wants to be Told He Has Big Muscles

CHOOSING TO HELP, follow, and love your husband in the way he needs to be loved is the hardest part of getting your husband more involved in family, homeschool, and your marriage.

Now, you need the secret weapon...the sure-fire ingredient to loving your husband and getting him more involved.

Here it is:

Hang on his arm and tell him that his muscles are big.

Actually, this summarizes the whole book. That's what helping, believe, encouraging, admiring, and desiring is. It's clinging to your husband and telling him his ideas are brilliant, his character sterling, his actions perfect, his dreams noble, his future bright, and HIS MUSCLES BIG.

That's it. I'm not kidding. If you put this into practice, it will transform your husband, your marriage, and your homeschool.

Here are some practical examples of how to do this:

* Your husband pulls into a parking space at the mall. Yes, it's too far out, but you keep your mouth shut and say, "This is a good spot." You've just proven to your husband that he is smart enough to find a parking space.

* You ask your husband's input in solving a dilemma that you're faced with. He gives his input and...you follow his advice, proving that you think he is smart and wise.

* Your husband gets the kids dressed for church like you asked. You see them and they look like they're part of the cast for a Charles Dickens' play. You say, "Thanks for getting them dressed, you did a great job." You've just proven to your husband that he is capable of doing simple tasks.

* Your husband gets the idea that he's going to help you with the dishes. He opens the dishwasher and does the unthinkable. He puts the cups where the bowls go. Instead of rushing in and moving them, you say, "Thanks a bunch honey. That sure makes my job easier." You've just proven to your husband that you NEED and appreciate his help.

* Your husband has just gotten home late from work. The kids are in bed, and he has missed out on the best God

has to offer. Instead of raking him over the coals for being late or ignoring him, you wrap your arms around him and thank him for working so hard to meet the needs of his family. You've just proven to him that you appreciate him.

* You catch your husband playing a game with the kids, reading a book to the youngest, or talking to your teenager. Tell him later, "You're such a good dad. Boy, the kids really love being with you." You've just proven to him that you believe in him.

* Your husband takes the trash out...after forgetting the last two weeks, and you give him a big kiss and say, "You know I really appreciate you taking out the trash. You're so strong and make it look easy." You've just proven to him that you admire him.

* Your husband finally fixes that "thing" you've been nagging him to fix for the last three months. You say, "Thank you so much for doing that. I know it was a big pain, but I could have never done that like you did." You've just proven to him that you view him as your stud, Mr. Fix-it.

* Before bed, your husband finds a note wrapped around his toothbrush that says, "I want you—now!" He goes to the bedroom and finds you wearing a skimpy little number that sends chills up his back. You've just proven to your husband that you desire him.

* Your husband has just yelled and sent your son to his bedroom without dinner. You come up to him and whisper, "Thanks for taking care of that so I didn't have to." You've just proven to him that you believe in him.

If you prove to your husband that you believe in him, admire him, desire him and then help him be what God wants him to be, and follow him come hell or high water, HE WILL BECOME MORE INVOLVED IN HOMESCHOOLING YOUR CHILDREN AND IN YOUR MARRIAGE.

If you hang on your husband's arm and tell him that his muscles are big, he will pull hard as the lead dog, he will treat you like a princess, slay dragons for you, and he will love you as you long to be loved.

Let's Talk

1. Which one of the examples on pages 90-92 can you most relate to?

2. Which one of the examples would be the hardest for YOU to implement?

3. When is the last time you told your husband that he has big muscles?

FOR THE REST OF YOUR LIFE
. . . .

Hang on your husband's arm and tell him that his muscles are big!

. . . .

Thank you for allowing me to be a part of what you're doing to raise up children for the KING. I know that what I've shared with you and what God asks of you can sometimes feel overwhelming, but I believe in you. I believe you can do the things we've talked about in this book.

You WILL find joy and fulfillment in being your husband's helper, follower, and encourager. Choose the best...

Choose the stem,

Todd

A Familyman Commercial

CAN I ASK a favor? Would you allow me to encourage your husband in "the important stuff?" I send out a short weekly email to thousands of dads across the country. I tell them to be good fathers and loving husbands, and encourage them to be more involved in their families (what do you know, just the things you want for him).

The great thing about it is that when I say these things, it doesn't come across as nagging. I'm just a struggling dad encouraging another struggling dad. I'll also give him links to fun pages, thought-provoking articles, and products that encourage him in the best job there is...fathering.

You can sign your husband up for the *Familyman Weekly* at www.familymanweb.com

---

"REMINDING DADS (AND MOMS) OF WHAT'S MOST IMPORTANT"

This phrase describes my life mission and the message that I bring to my listening and reading audiences. I would be delighted to hear from you. Contact me at:
www.familymanweb.com.

Familyman ministries

"Reminding dads of what's most important"